INTRODUCTION

Embroidery—the art of applying decorative motifs to fabric with a needle and thread—has been around for centuries and has roots in nearly every culture. Despite its long history, this versatile craft has managed to evolve with the times and is still immensely popular today for everything from clothing repairs to artwork and home décor. In addition to needles and thread, embroiderers often use hoops to keep the fabric taut as they stitch, but modern crafters have started working stitches on unexpected materials like tennis rackets and even metal. No matter what medium is used, it all comes back to the stitch.

Our embroidery pocket guide provides you with general information about fabric, thread, and transferring designs to help you get started, as well as detailed diagrams for a wide variety of stitches. The easy-to-follow illustrations will have you hand embroidering new stitches in no time. Whether you are new to the world of embroidery or already a pro, this guide is a great resource to add to your toolbox; plus, it is compact and perfect for crafting on the go!

Table of Contents

CROSS STITCHES

Basic

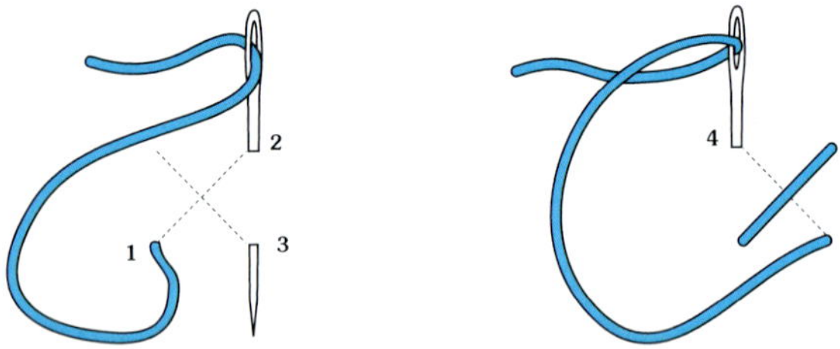

Double

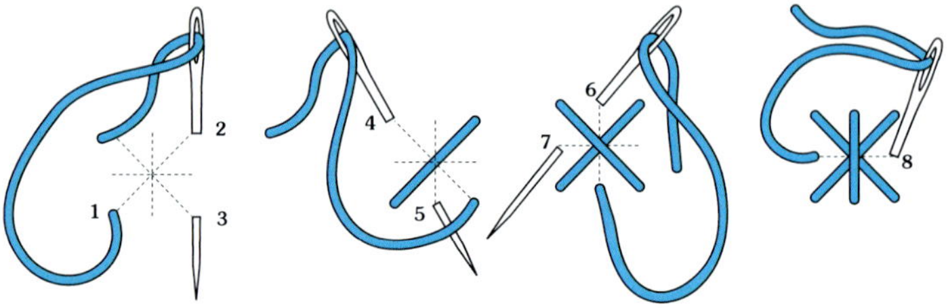

Herringbone

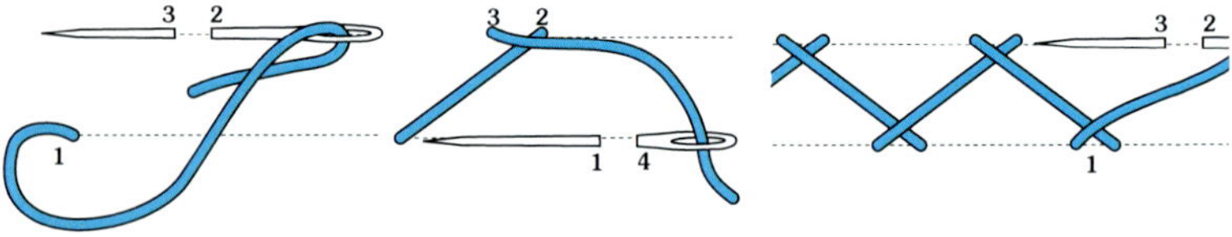

Closed Herringbone

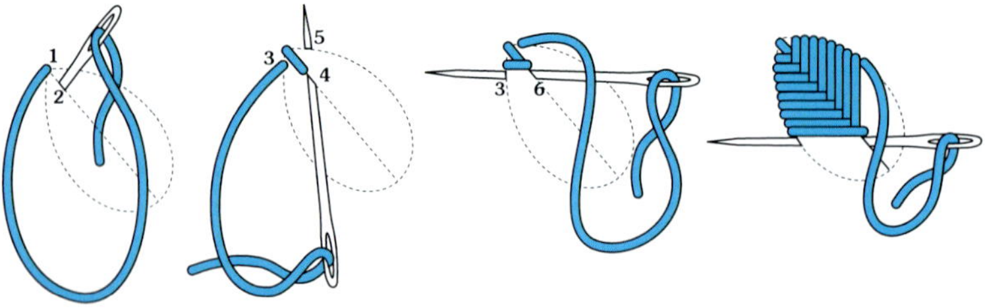

Vandyke

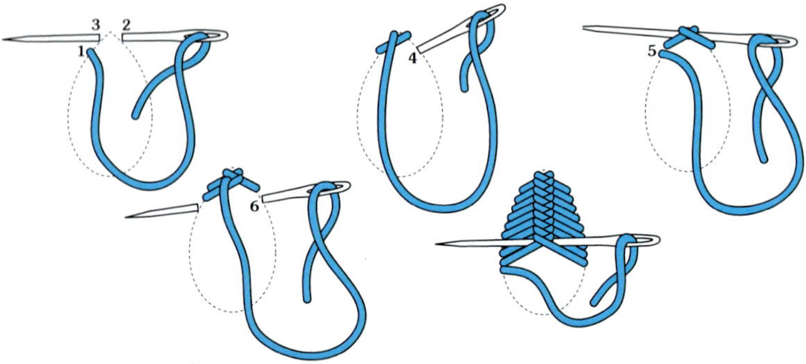

FEATHERSTITCHES

Basic

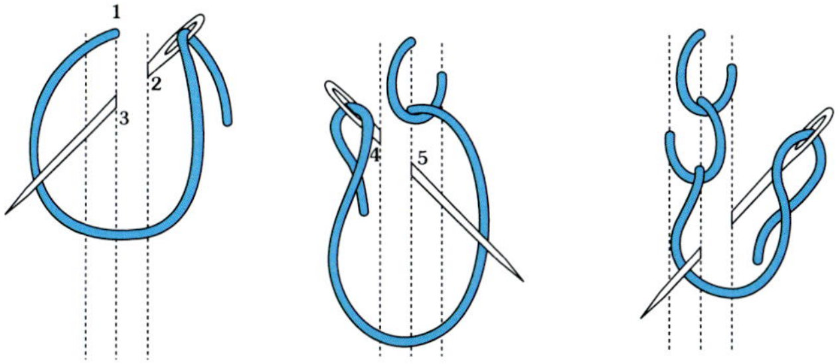

Double

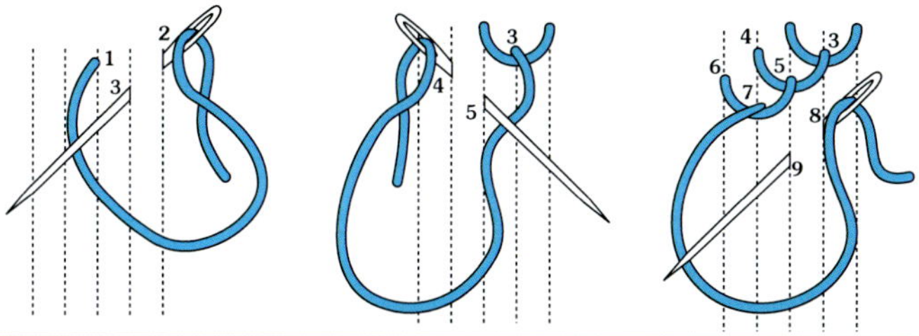

Open Cretan

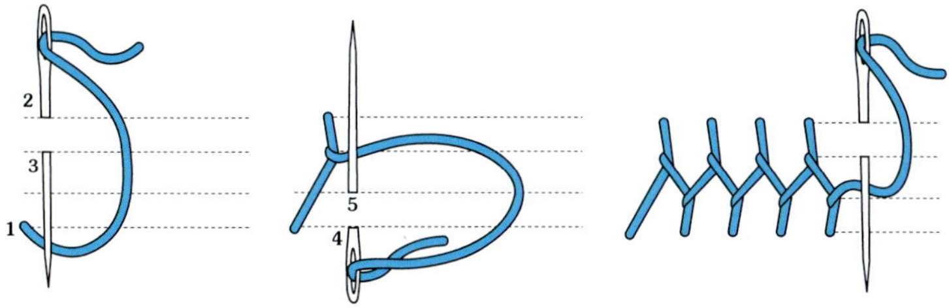

Closed Cretan

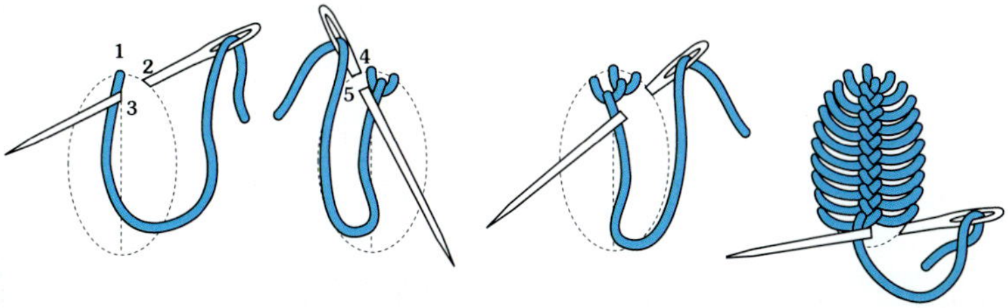

Fishbone

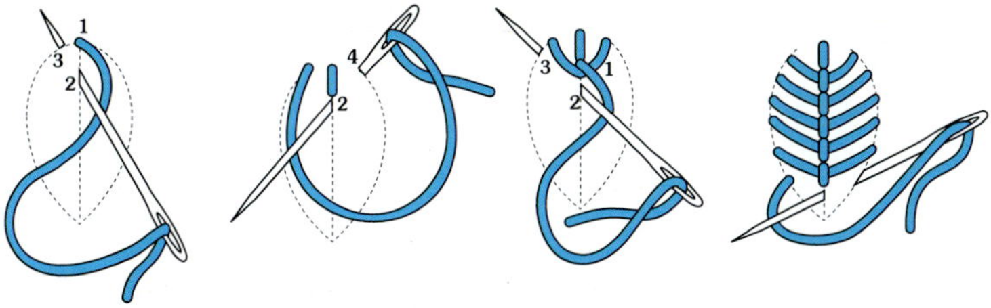

FILLING STITCHES

Seeding

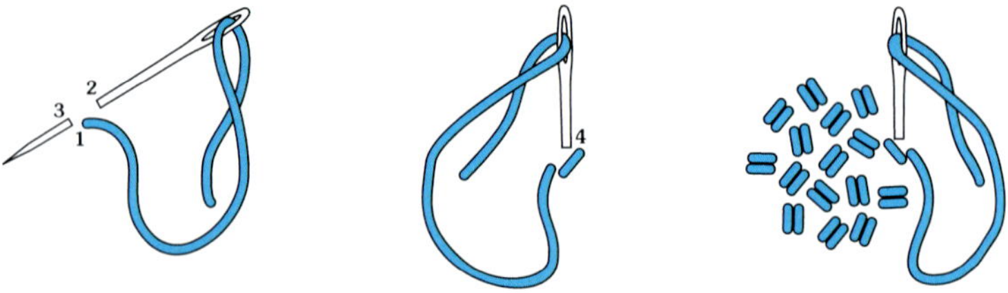

French Knot

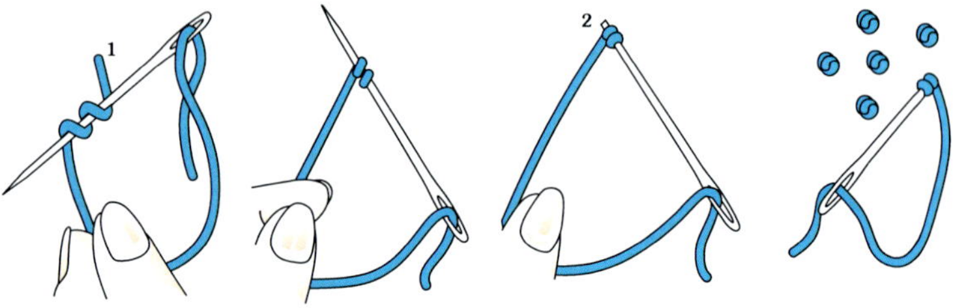

Bullion Knot

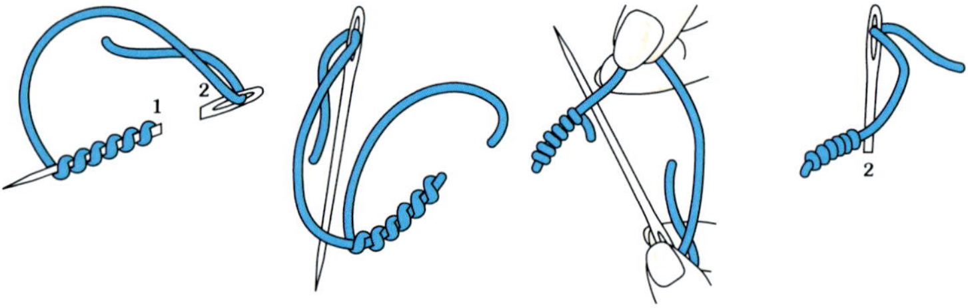

Fly

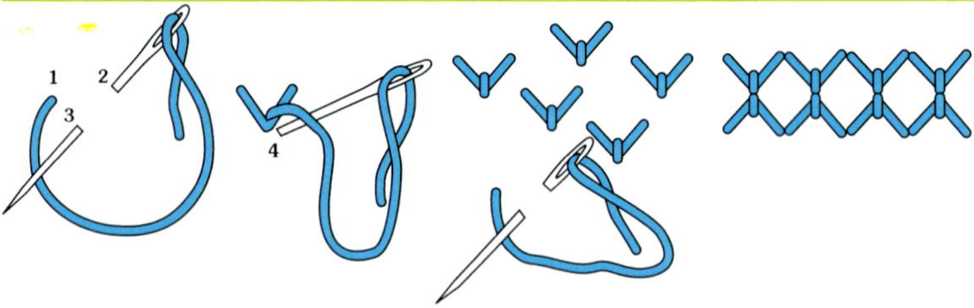

Sheaf

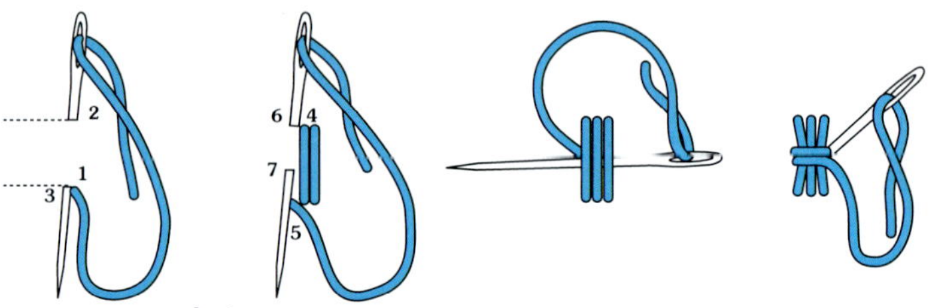

RUNNING STITCHES

Basic

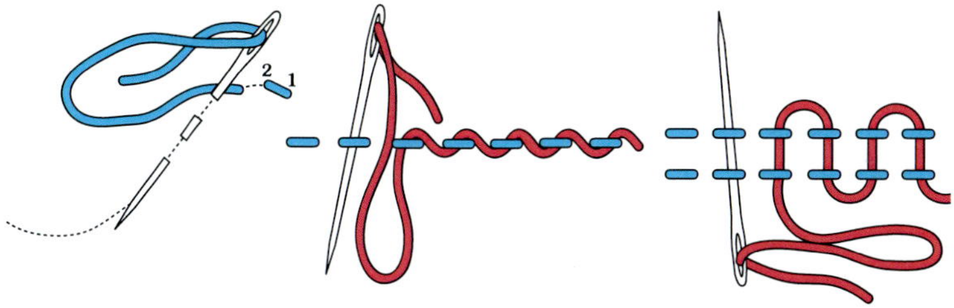

Darning

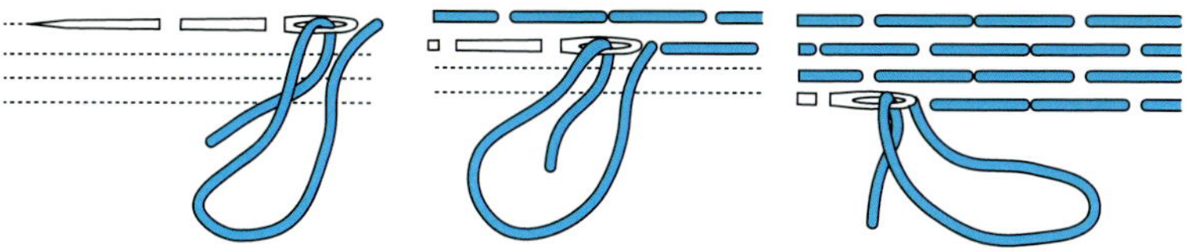

Holbein or Double

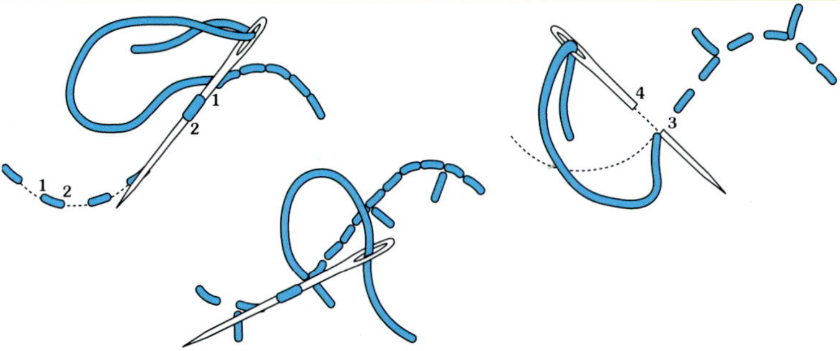

Double Darning

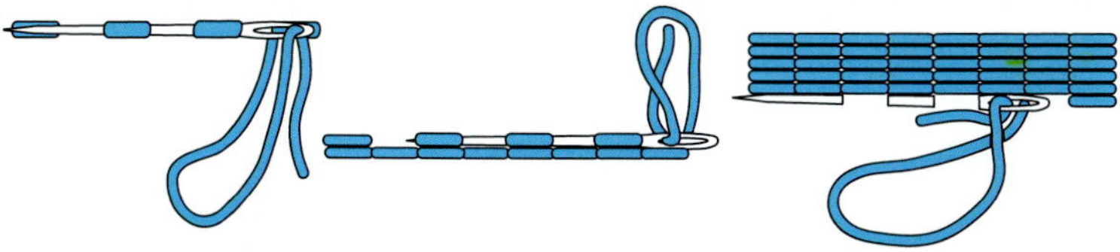

Japanese Darning

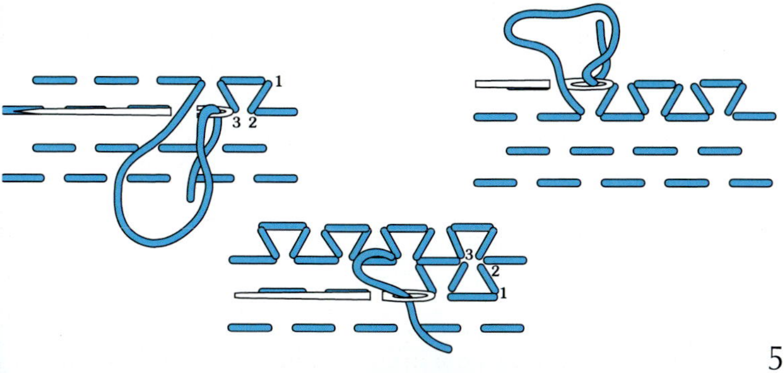

SATIN STITCHES

Basic

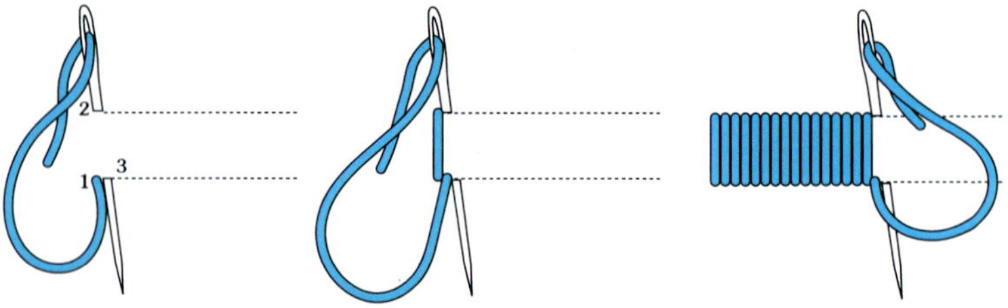

Padded

Encroaching

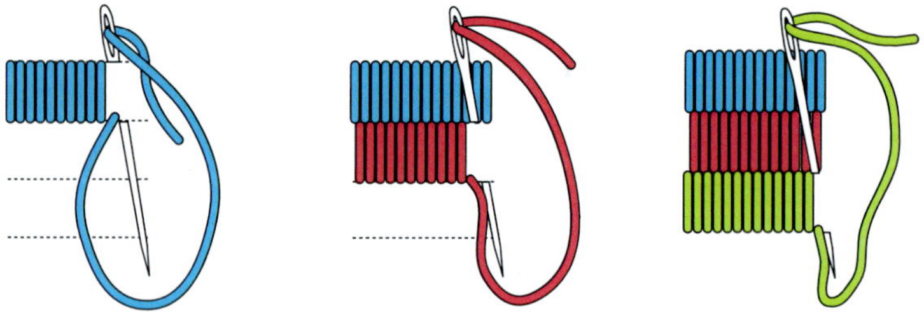

Long and Short

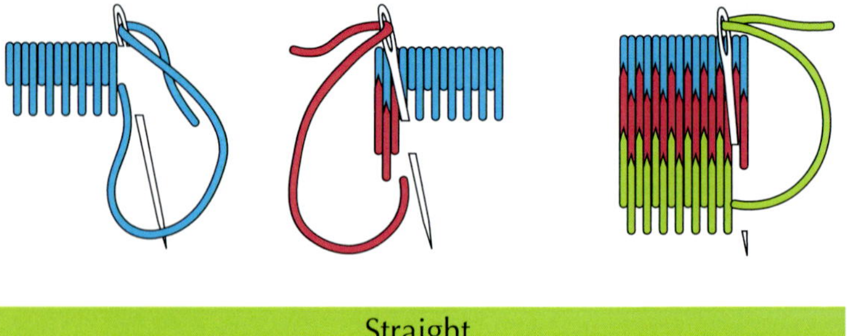

Straight

WEAVING STITCHES

Basic

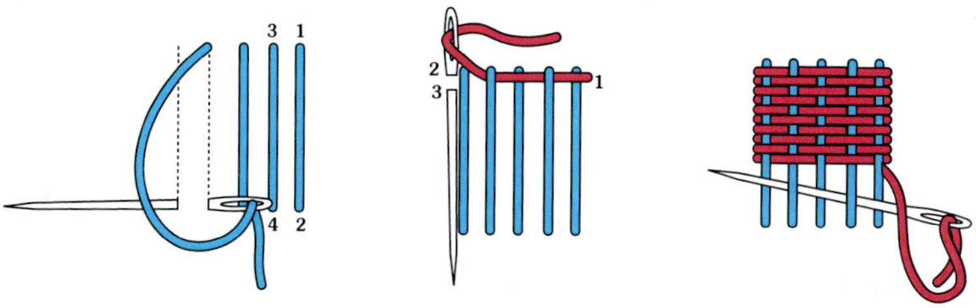

Raised Needleweaving

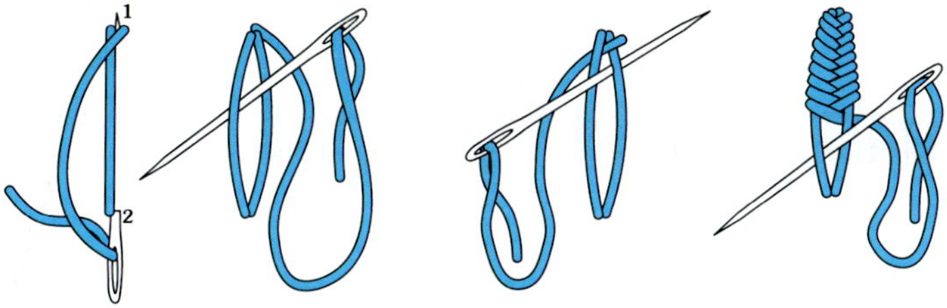

Cloud Filling

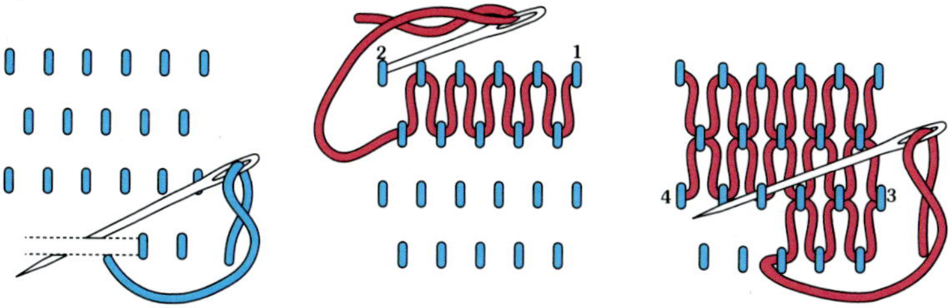

Spider Web

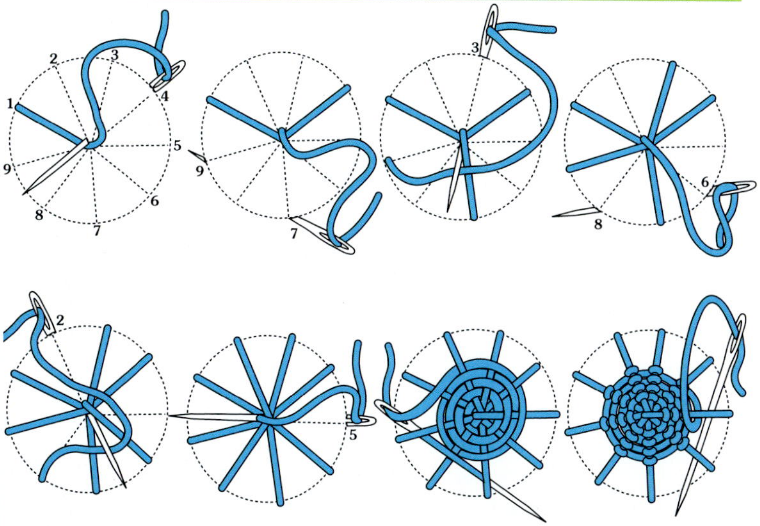

BACKSTITCHES

Basic

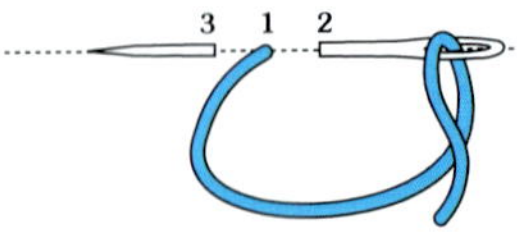

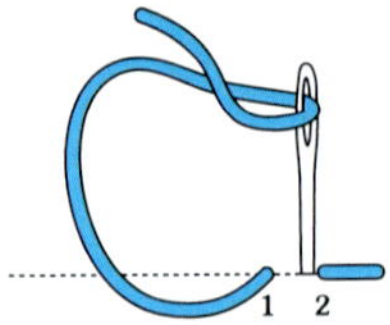

Single- or Double-threaded

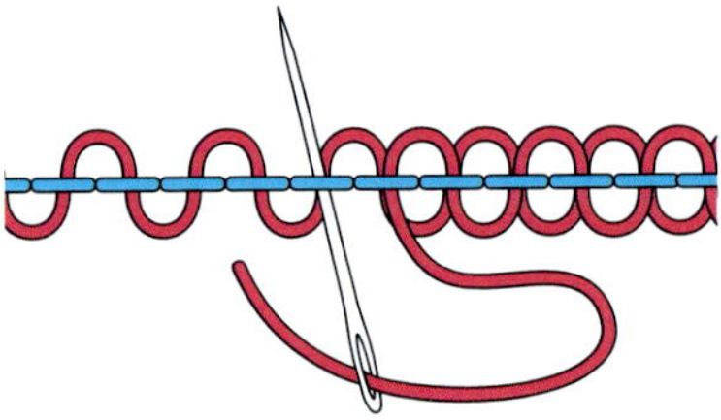

Pekinese

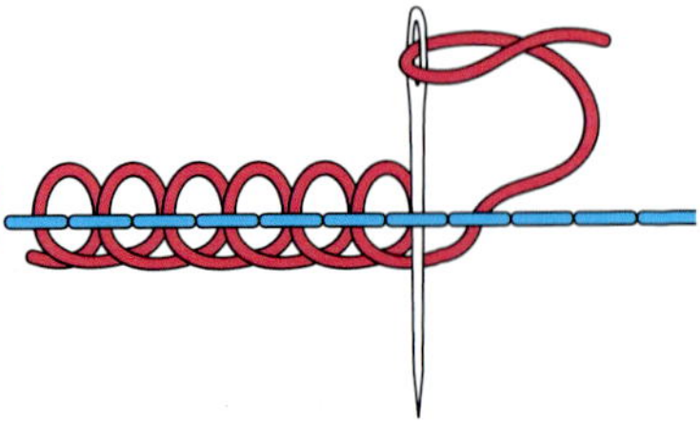

Chevron

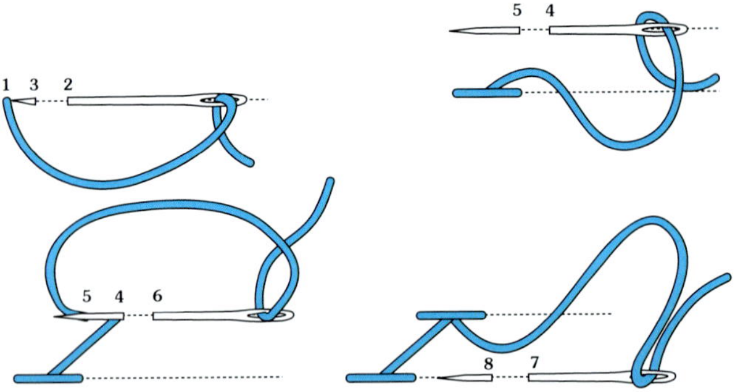

Stem

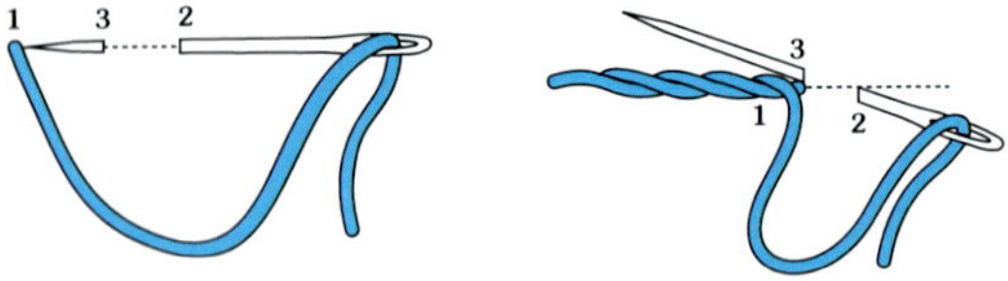

Turkey Work

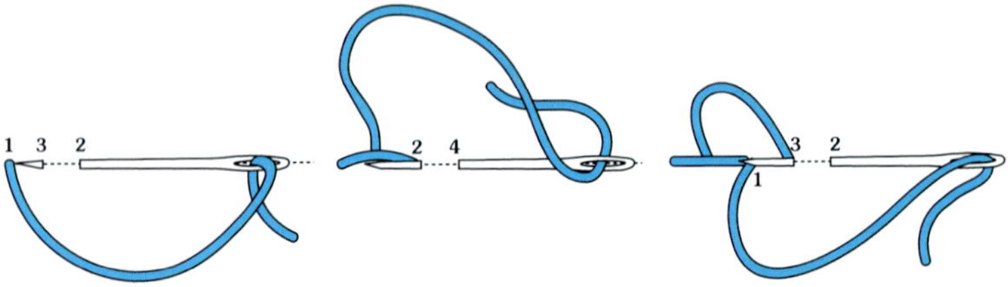

BLANKET STITCHES

Basic

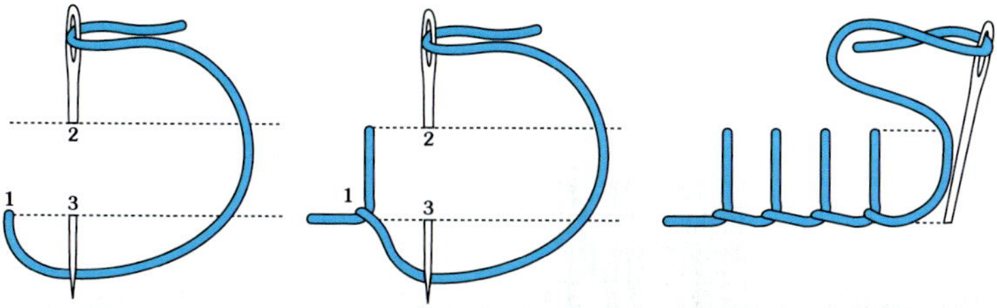

Long and Short

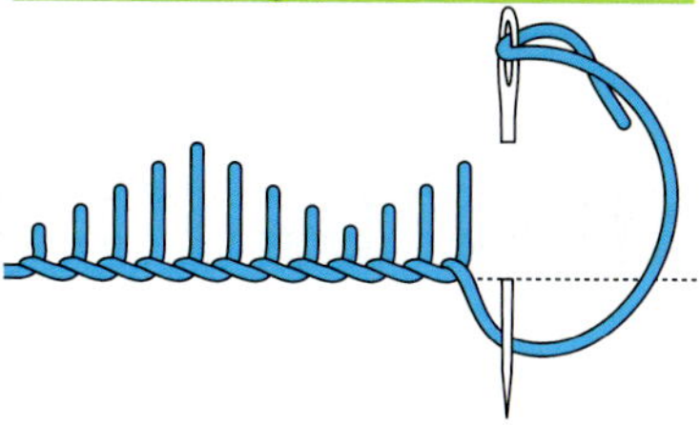

Double

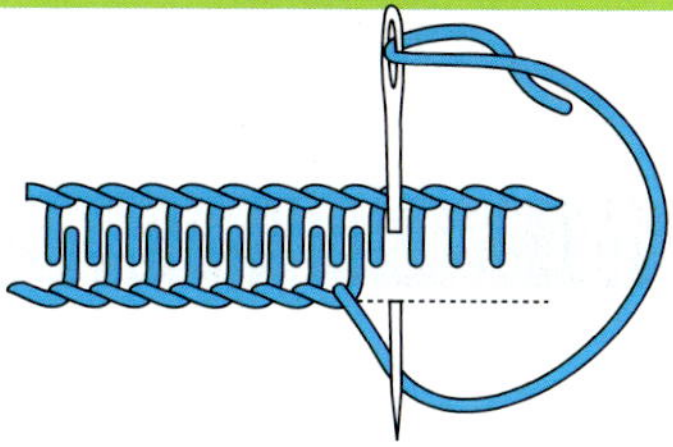

Basic Buttonhole

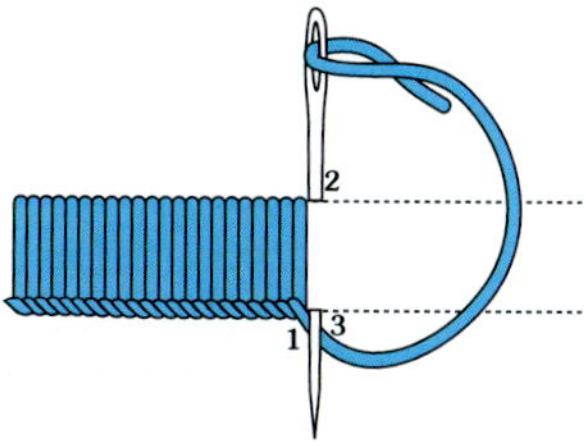

Buttonhole Wheel

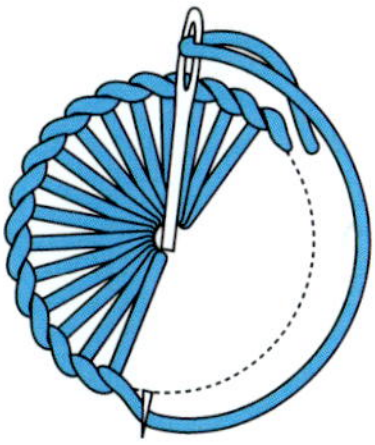

Closed Buttonhole

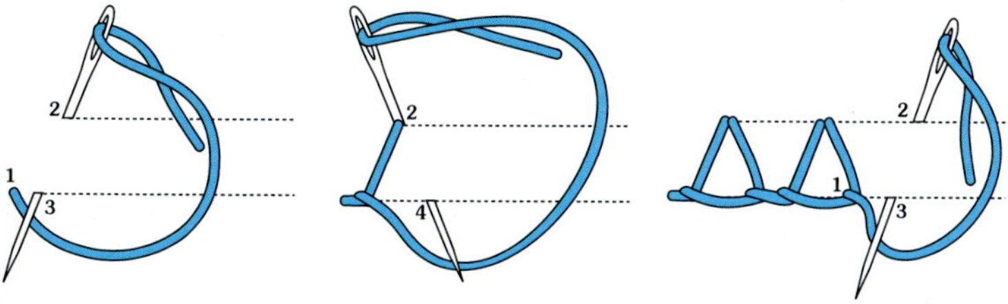

Knotted

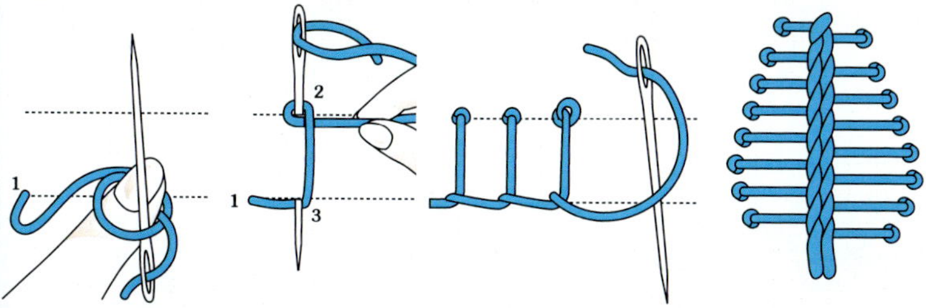

CHAIN STITCHES

Basic

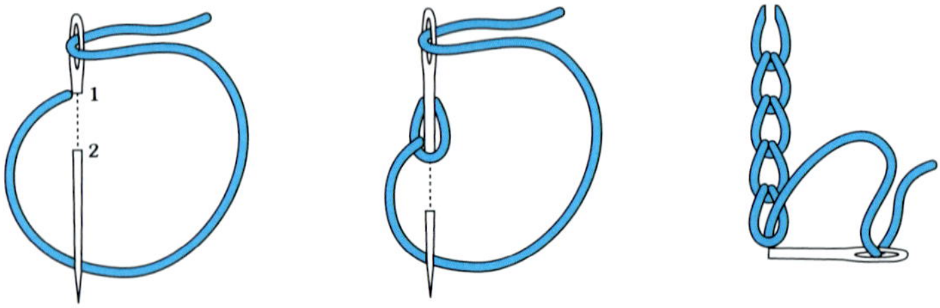

Lazy Daisy

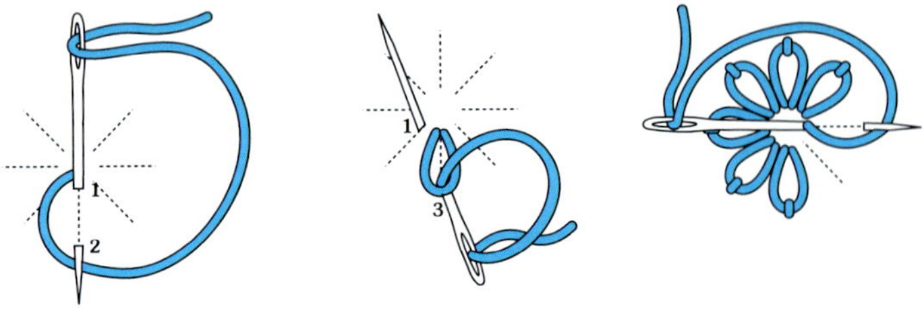

Zigzag

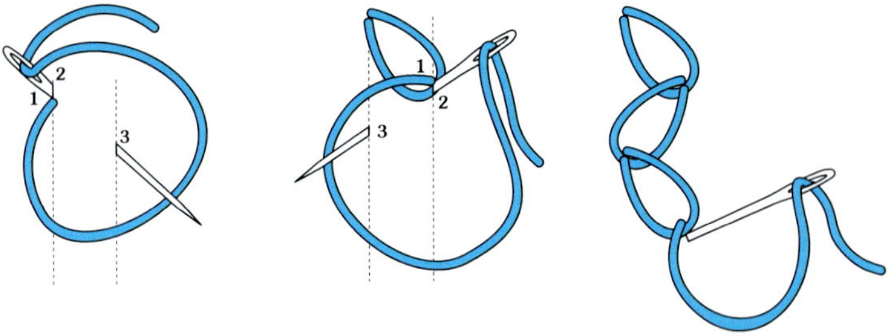

Twisted

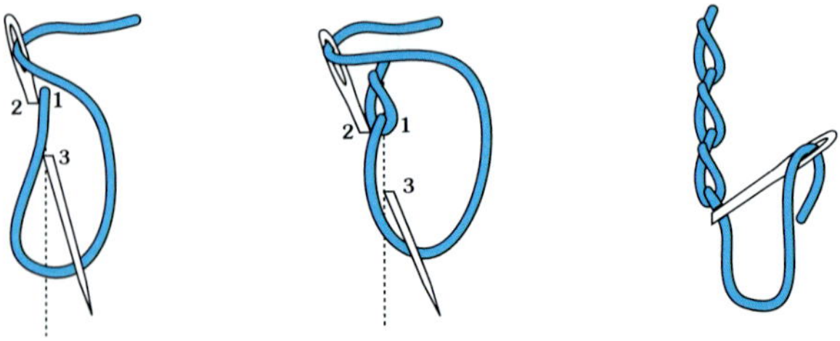

Square

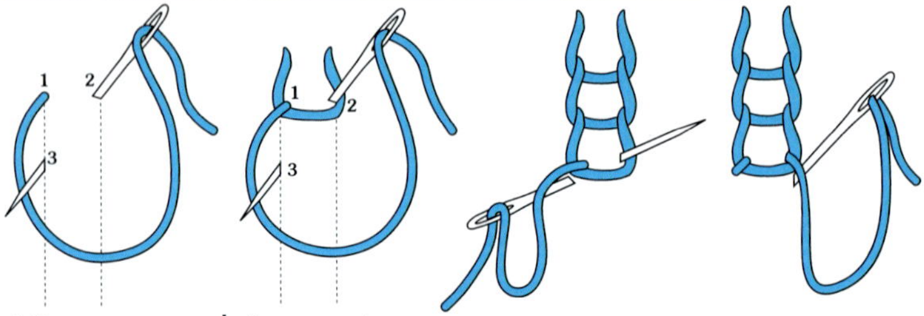

COUCHING STITCHES

Basic

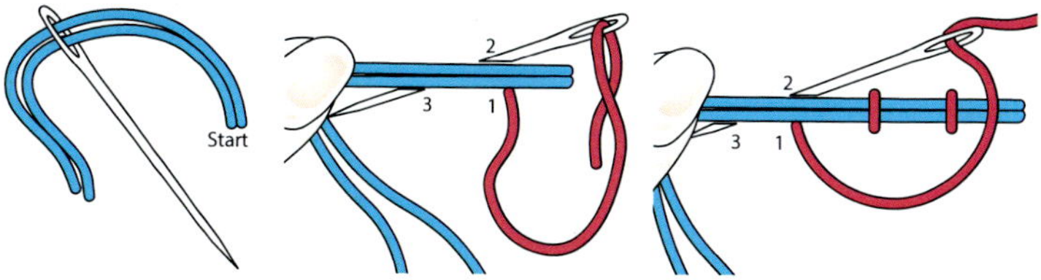

Bokhara

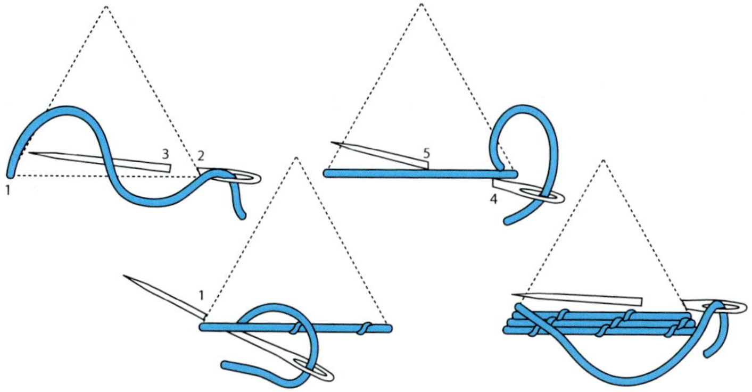

Roumanian

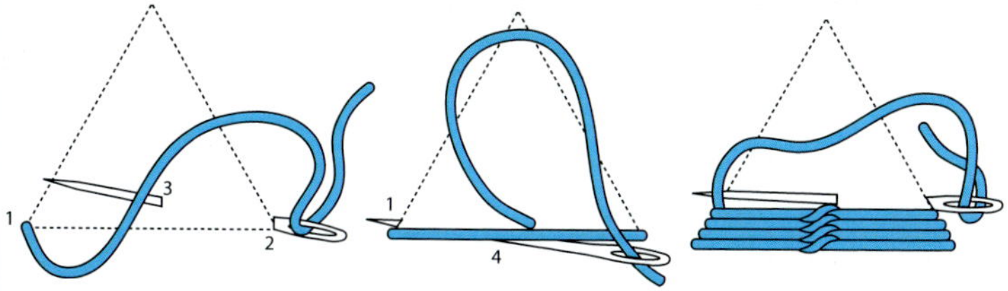

Circular

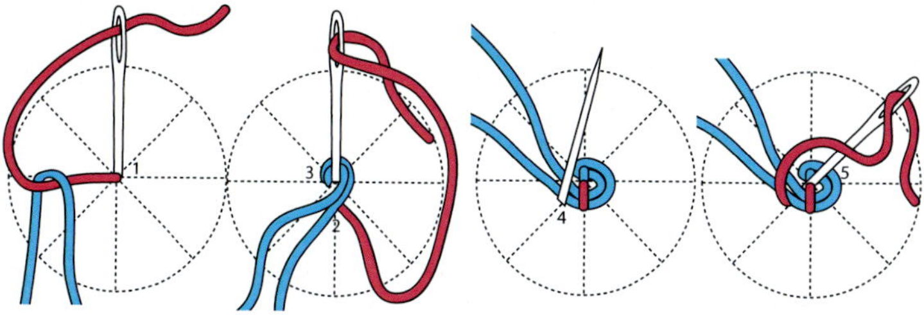

Fabrics	Floss/Yarns	Needles
Wools, Velvets	Embroidery Floss, Silk Ribbon	Crewel No. 6,7,8 or Chenille No. 18-24
Cottons, Linens	Embroidery Floss, Persian Wool, Perle Cotton, Tapestry Wool	Crewel No. 4,5,6,7 or Tapestry No. 20 or 22
Satins	Embroidery Floss, Embroidery Thread, Perle Cotton	Crewel No. 4,5,6,7,8
Lightweight Silks	Embroidery Floss, Embroidery Thread	Crewel No. 6,7,8
Knits, Loosely Woven Fabrics	Persian Wool, Crewel Yarns	Chenille No. 18 or 20 or Tapestry No. 13,16
Canvas for Needlepoint or Cross Stitch	Embroidery Floss, Embroidery Thread, Perle Cotton, Tapestry Wool	Tapestry No. 24 or 26 or Chenille No. 18-24

Preparing yarns or floss: Separate the skein of yarn or floss into the number of ply or strands needed for the project. The length of yarn or floss should be no longer than 18".

Transferring designs: An iron-on transfer may be made from a design by placing tracing paper over the design and drawing over the lines with an iron-on transfer pencil. Dressmaker's carbon paper may also be used by placing carbon paper between design and fabric, then drawing over lines with a dull pencil.

To begin stitching:
Hold end of yarn or floss on wrong side of fabric; work several stitches over yarn or floss end. If some stitching has already been done, slide needle under wrong side of stitches.

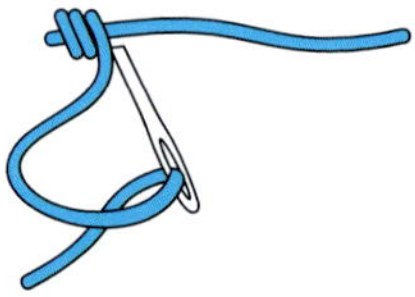

To end stitching:
Slide needle under wrong side of stitches and cut yarn or floss end.

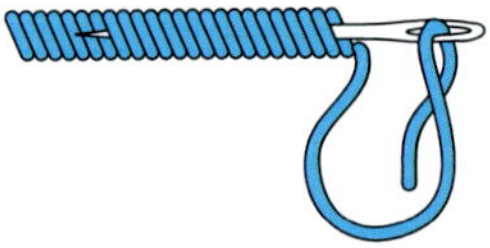

For numbered stitch diagrams, come up at odd numbers and go down at even numbers.